FOR KIDS

Gratitude Journal

THIS BOOK BELONGS TO

_____

_____

_____

Date : ...... / ...... / ......

Mon Tue Wed Thu Fri Sat Sun
○   ○   ○   ○   ○   ○   ○

My level of happiness

Today I'm thankful for

_____
_____
_____
_____
_____

Something awesome that happened today

_____
_____
_____

Something I learned today

_____
_____
_____
_____

Date : .... / .... / ....

Mon Tue Wed Thu Fri Sat Sun
○   ○   ○   ○   ○   ○   ○

My level of happiness

Today I'm thankful for

_____
_____
_____
_____
_____

Something awesome that happened today

_____
_____
_____

Something I learned today

_____
_____
_____
_____

Date : ...... / ...... / ......

Mon Tue Wed Thu Fri Sat Sun
○   ○   ○   ○   ○   ○   ○

My level of happiness

Today I'm thankful for

Something awesome that happened today

Something I learned today

Date : .... / .... / ....

Mon Tue Wed Thu Fri Sat Sun
○   ○   ○   ○   ○   ○   ○

My level of happiness

Today I'm thankful for

_____
_____
_____
_____
_____
_____

Something awesome that happened today

_____
_____
_____
_____

Something I learned today

_____
_____
_____
_____

Date : ...... / ...... / ......

Mon Tue Wed Thu Fri Sat Sun
○   ○   ○   ○   ○   ○   ○

My level of happiness

Today I'm thankful for

_____

_____

_____

_____

_____

Something awesome that happened today

_____

_____

_____

Something I learned today

_____

_____

_____

_____

Date : ...... / ...... / ......

Mon Tue Wed Thu Fri Sat Sun
○   ○   ○   ○   ○   ○   ○

My level of happiness

Today I'm thankful for

_____
_____
_____
_____
_____

Something awesome that happened today

_____
_____
_____

Something I learned today

_____
_____
_____
_____

Date : ...... / ...... / ......

Mon Tue Wed Thu Fri Sat Sun
○   ○   ○   ○   ○   ○   ○

My level of happiness

Today I'm thankful for

_____
_____
_____
_____
_____

Something awesome that happened today

_____
_____
_____

Something I learned today

_____
_____
_____
_____

Date : ...... / ...... / ......

Mon Tue Wed Thu Fri Sat Sun
○   ○   ○   ○   ○   ○   ○

My level of happiness

Today I'm thankful for

_____
_____
_____
_____
_____

Something awesome that happened today

_____
_____
_____

Something I learned today

_____
_____
_____
_____

Date : ...... / ...... / ......

Mon Tue Wed Thu Fri Sat Sun
◯   ◯   ◯   ◯   ◯   ◯   ◯

My level of happiness

Today I'm thankful for

Something awesome that happened today

Something I learned today

Date : ...... / ...... / ......

Mon Tue Wed Thu Fri Sat Sun
○   ○   ○   ○   ○   ○   ○

My level of happiness

Today I'm thankful for

_____
_____
_____
_____
_____

Something awesome that happened today

_____
_____
_____

Something I learned today

_____
_____
_____
_____

Date : .... / .... / ....

Mon Tue Wed Thu Fri Sat Sun
○ ○ ○ ○ ○ ○ ○

Today I'm thankful for

_____
_____
_____
_____
_____

Something awesome that happened today

_____
_____
_____

Something I learned today

_____
_____
_____
_____

Date : .... / .... / ....

Mon Tue Wed Thu Fri Sat Sun
○   ○   ○   ○   ○   ○   ○

My level of happiness

Today I'm thankful for

_____
_____
_____
_____
_____

Something awesome that happened today

_____
_____
_____

Something I learned today

_____
_____
_____
_____

Date : ...... / ...... / ......

Mon Tue Wed Thu Fri Sat Sun
○   ○   ○   ○   ○   ○   ○

My level of happiness

Today I'm thankful for

_____
_____
_____
_____
_____

Something awesome that happened today

_____
_____
_____

Something I learned today

_____
_____
_____
_____

Date : ...... / ...... / ......

Mon Tue Wed Thu Fri Sat Sun
 ○   ○   ○   ○   ○   ○   ○

My level of happiness

Today I'm thankful for

_____
_____
_____
_____
_____
_____

Something awesome that happened today

_____
_____
_____

Something I learned today

_____
_____
_____
_____

Date : ...... / ...... / ......

Mon Tue Wed Thu Fri Sat Sun
○ ○ ○ ○ ○ ○ ○

My level of happiness

Today I'm thankful for

_____
_____
_____
_____
_____

Something awesome that happened today

_____
_____
_____

Something I learned today

_____
_____
_____
_____

Date : ...... / ...... / ......

Mon Tue Wed Thu Fri Sat Sun
○   ○   ○   ○   ○   ○   ○

My level of happiness

Today I'm thankful for

_____

_____

_____

_____

_____

Something awesome that happened today

_____

_____

_____

Something I learned today

_____

_____

_____

_____

Date : ...... / ...... / ......

Mon Tue Wed Thu Fri Sat Sun
 ○   ○   ○   ○   ○   ○   ○

My level of happiness

Today I'm thankful for

_____
_____
_____
_____
_____

Something awesome that happened today

_____
_____
_____
_____

Something I learned today

_____
_____
_____
_____

Date : ...... / ...... / ......

Mon Tue Wed Thu Fri Sat Sun
○ ○ ○ ○ ○ ○ ○

My level of happiness

Today I'm thankful for

_____
_____
_____
_____
_____

Something awesome that happened today

_____
_____
_____

Something I learned today

_____
_____
_____
_____

Date : ...... / ...... / ......

Mon Tue Wed Thu Fri Sat Sun
○ ○ ○ ○ ○ ○ ○

My level of happiness

Today I'm thankful for

_____
_____
_____
_____
_____

Something awesome that happened today

_____
_____
_____

Something I learned today

_____
_____
_____
_____

Date : .... / .... / ....

Mon Tue Wed Thu Fri Sat Sun
○   ○   ○   ○   ○   ○   ○

My level of happiness

Today I'm thankful for

_____

_____

_____

_____

_____

Something awesome that happened today

_____

_____

_____

_____

Something I learned today

_____

_____

_____

_____

Date : ...... / ...... / ......

Mon Tue Wed Thu Fri Sat Sun
○   ○   ○   ○   ○   ○   ○

My level of happiness

Today I'm thankful for

_____

_____

_____

_____

_____

Something awesome that happened today

_____

_____

_____

Something I learned today

_____

_____

_____

_____

Date : ...... / ...... / ......

Mon Tue Wed Thu Fri Sat Sun
○   ○   ○   ○   ○   ○   ○

My level of happiness

Today I'm thankful for

_____
_____
_____
_____
_____

Something awesome that happened today

_____
_____
_____

Something I learned today

_____
_____
_____
_____

Date : ...... / ...... / ......

Mon Tue Wed Thu Fri Sat Sun
○ ○ ○ ○ ○ ○ ○

My level of happiness

Today I'm thankful for

_____
_____
_____
_____
_____

Something awesome that happened today

_____
_____
_____

Something I learned today

_____
_____
_____
_____

Date : ...... / ...... / ......

Mon Tue Wed Thu Fri Sat Sun
○   ○   ○   ○   ○   ○   ○

My level of happiness

Today I'm thankful for

_____
_____
_____
_____
_____

Something awesome that happened today

_____
_____
_____

Something I learned today

_____
_____
_____
_____

Date : ...... / ...... / ......

Mon Tue Wed Thu Fri Sat Sun
◯ ◯ ◯ ◯ ◯ ◯ ◯

My level of happiness

Today I'm thankful for

_____
_____
_____
_____
_____

Something awesome that happened today

_____
_____
_____

Something I learned today

_____
_____
_____
_____

Date : ...... / ...... / ......

Mon Tue Wed Thu Fri Sat Sun
○   ○   ○   ○   ○   ○   ○

My level of happiness

Today I'm thankful for

_____
_____
_____
_____
_____

Something awesome that happened today

_____
_____
_____

Something I learned today

_____
_____
_____
_____

Date : ...... / ...... / ......

Mon Tue Wed Thu Fri Sat Sun
○ ○ ○ ○ ○ ○ ○

My level of happiness

Today I'm thankful for

_____
_____
_____
_____
_____

Something awesome that happened today

_____
_____
_____

Something I learned today

_____
_____
_____
_____

Date : ...... / ...... / ......

Mon Tue Wed Thu Fri Sat Sun
○ ○ ○ ○ ○ ○ ○

My level of happiness

Today I'm thankful for

_____
_____
_____
_____
_____

Something awesome that happened today

_____
_____
_____

Something I learned today

_____
_____
_____
_____

Date : .... / .... / ....

Mon Tue Wed Thu Fri Sat Sun
 ○   ○   ○   ○   ○   ○   ○

My level of happiness

Today I'm thankful for

_____

_____

_____

_____

_____

Something awesome that happened today

_____

_____

_____

Something I learned today

_____

_____

_____

_____

Date : ...... / ...... / ......

Mon Tue Wed Thu Fri Sat Sun
○ ○ ○ ○ ○ ○ ○

My level of happiness

Today I'm thankful for

_____
_____
_____
_____
_____

Something awesome that happened today

_____
_____
_____

Something I learned today

_____
_____
_____
_____

Date : .... / .... / ....

Mon Tue Wed Thu Fri Sat Sun
○ ○ ○ ○ ○ ○ ○

Today I'm thankful for

_____
_____
_____
_____
_____

Something awesome that happened today

_____
_____
_____

Something I learned today

_____
_____
_____
_____

Date : ...... / ...... / ......

Mon Tue Wed Thu Fri Sat Sun
○ ○ ○ ○ ○ ○ ○

My level of happiness

Today I'm thankful for

_____
_____
_____
_____
_____

Something awesome that happened today

_____
_____
_____

Something I learned today

_____
_____
_____
_____

Date : ...... / ...... / ......

Mon Tue Wed Thu Fri Sat Sun
○   ○   ○   ○   ○   ○   ○

My level of happiness

Today I'm thankful for

Something awesome that happened today

Something I learned today

Date : ...... / ...... / ......

Mon Tue Wed Thu Fri Sat Sun
 ○   ○   ○   ○   ○   ○   ○

My level of happiness

Today I'm thankful for

_____

_____

_____

_____

_____

Something awesome that happened today

_____

_____

_____

Something I learned today

_____

_____

_____

_____

Date : .... / .... / ....

Mon Tue Wed Thu Fri Sat Sun
○ ○ ○ ○ ○ ○ ○

My level of happiness

Today I'm thankful for

_____
_____
_____
_____
_____

Something awesome that happened today

_____
_____
_____

Something I learned today

_____
_____
_____
_____

Date : ...... / ...... / ......

Mon Tue Wed Thu Fri Sat Sun
○   ○   ○   ○   ○   ○   ○

My level of happiness

Today I'm thankful for

Something awesome that happened today

Something I learned today

Date : .... / .... / ....

Mon Tue Wed Thu Fri Sat Sun
○   ○   ○   ○   ○   ○   ○

My level of happiness

Today I'm thankful for

_____

_____

_____

_____

_____

Something awesome that happened today

_____

_____

_____

Something I learned today

_____

_____

_____

_____

Date : ...... / ...... / ......

Mon Tue Wed Thu Fri Sat Sun
○   ○   ○   ○   ○   ○   ○

My level of happiness

Today I'm thankful for

_____
_____
_____
_____
_____

Something awesome that happened today

_____
_____
_____

Something I learned today

_____
_____
_____
_____

Date : ...... / ...... / ......

Mon Tue Wed Thu Fri Sat Sun
○   ○   ○   ○   ○   ○   ○

My level of happiness

Today I'm thankful for

Something awesome that happened today

Something I learned today

Date : ...... / ...... / ......

Mon Tue Wed Thu Fri Sat Sun
○   ○   ○   ○   ○   ○   ○

My level of happiness

Today I'm thankful for

_____
_____
_____
_____
_____

Something awesome that happened today

_____
_____
_____

Something I learned today

_____
_____
_____
_____

Date : ...... / ...... / ......

Mon Tue Wed Thu Fri Sat Sun
○ ○ ○ ○ ○ ○ ○

My level of happiness

Today I'm thankful for

_____
_____
_____
_____
_____

Something awesome that happened today

_____
_____
_____

Something I learned today

_____
_____
_____
_____

Date : ...... / ...... / ......

Mon Tue Wed Thu Fri Sat Sun
○   ○   ○   ○   ○   ○   ○

My level of happiness

Today I'm thankful for

_____
_____
_____
_____
_____

Something awesome that happened today

_____
_____
_____

Something I learned today

_____
_____
_____
_____

Date : ...... / ...... / ......

Mon Tue Wed Thu Fri Sat Sun
○ ○ ○ ○ ○ ○ ○

My level of happiness

Today I'm thankful for

Something awesome that happened today

Something I learned today

Date : ...... / ...... / ......

Mon Tue Wed Thu Fri Sat Sun
○   ○   ○   ○   ○   ○   ○

My level of happiness

Today I'm thankful for

_____
_____
_____
_____
_____

Something awesome that happened today

_____
_____
_____

Something I learned today

_____
_____
_____
_____

Date : ...... / ...... / ......

Mon Tue Wed Thu Fri Sat Sun
○   ○   ○   ○   ○   ○   ○

My level of happiness

Today I'm thankful for

_____
_____
_____
_____
_____

Something awesome that happened today

_____
_____
_____

Something I learned today

_____
_____
_____
_____

Date : ...... / ...... / ......

Mon Tue Wed Thu Fri Sat Sun
○ ○ ○ ○ ○ ○ ○

My level of happiness

Today I'm thankful for

_____
_____
_____
_____
_____

Something awesome that happened today

_____
_____
_____

Something I learned today

_____
_____
_____
_____

Date : .... / .... / ....

Mon Tue Wed Thu Fri Sat Sun
○   ○   ○   ○   ○   ○   ○

My level of happiness

Today I'm thankful for

_____
_____
_____
_____
_____

Something awesome that happened today

_____
_____
_____

Something I learned today

_____
_____
_____
_____

Date : ...... / ...... / ......

Mon Tue Wed Thu Fri Sat Sun
○   ○   ○   ○   ○   ○   ○

My level of happiness

Today I'm thankful for

_____
_____
_____
_____
_____

Something awesome that happened today

_____
_____
_____

Something I learned today

_____
_____
_____
_____

Date : ...... / ...... / ......

Mon Tue Wed Thu Fri Sat Sun
○   ○   ○   ○   ○   ○   ○

My level of happiness

Today I'm thankful for

Something awesome that happened today

Something I learned today

Date : ...... / ...... / ......

Mon Tue Wed Thu Fri Sat Sun
○   ○   ○   ○   ○   ○   ○

My level of happiness

Today I'm thankful for

_____
_____
_____
_____
_____

Something awesome that happened today

_____
_____
_____
_____

Something I learned today

_____
_____
_____
_____

Date : ...... / ...... / ......

Mon Tue Wed Thu Fri Sat Sun
◯   ◯   ◯   ◯   ◯   ◯   ◯

My level of happiness

Today I'm thankful for

_____
_____
_____
_____
_____
_____

Something awesome that happened today

_____
_____
_____
_____

Something I learned today

_____
_____
_____
_____

Date : ...... / ...... / ......

Mon Tue Wed Thu Fri Sat Sun
◯   ◯   ◯   ◯   ◯   ◯   ◯

My level of happiness

Today I'm thankful for

_____
_____
_____
_____
_____

Something awesome that happened today

_____
_____
_____

Something I learned today

_____
_____
_____
_____

Date : ...... / ...... / ......

Mon Tue Wed Thu Fri Sat Sun
◯   ◯   ◯   ◯   ◯   ◯   ◯

My level of happiness

Today I'm thankful for

Something awesome that happened today

Something I learned today

Date : ...... / ...... / ......

Mon Tue Wed Thu Fri Sat Sun
○ ○ ○ ○ ○ ○ ○

My level of happiness

Today I'm thankful for

_____

_____

_____

_____

_____

Something awesome that happened today

_____

_____

_____

_____

Something I learned today

_____

_____

_____

_____

Date : ...... / ...... / ......

Mon Tue Wed Thu Fri Sat Sun
○   ○   ○   ○   ○   ○   ○

My level of happiness

Today I'm thankful for

Something awesome that happened today

Something I learned today

Date : ...... / ...... / ......

Mon Tue Wed Thu Fri Sat Sun
○ ○ ○ ○ ○ ○ ○

My level of happiness

Today I'm thankful for

_____
_____
_____
_____
_____

Something awesome that happened today

_____
_____
_____

Something I learned today

_____
_____
_____
_____

Date : ...... / ...... / ......

Mon Tue Wed Thu Fri Sat Sun
○   ○   ○   ○   ○   ○   ○

My level of happiness

Today I'm thankful for

_____

_____

_____

_____

_____

Something awesome that happened today

_____

_____

_____

Something I learned today

_____

_____

_____

_____

Date : .... / .... / ....

Mon Tue Wed Thu Fri Sat Sun
○ ○ ○ ○ ○ ○ ○

My level of happiness

Today I'm thankful for

_____
_____
_____
_____
_____

Something awesome that happened today

_____
_____
_____

Something I learned today

_____
_____
_____
_____

Date : .... / .... / ....

Mon Tue Wed Thu Fri Sat Sun
○   ○   ○   ○   ○   ○   ○

My level of happiness

Today I'm thankful for

_____
_____
_____
_____
_____
_____

Something awesome that happened today

_____
_____
_____

Something I learned today

_____
_____
_____
_____

Date : ...... / ...... / ......

Mon Tue Wed Thu Fri Sat Sun
○   ○   ○   ○   ○   ○   ○

My level of happiness

Today I'm thankful for

Something awesome that happened today

Something I learned today

Date : ...... / ...... / ......

Mon Tue Wed Thu Fri Sat Sun
○ ○ ○ ○ ○ ○ ○

My level of happiness

Today I'm thankful for

_____
_____
_____
_____
_____

Something awesome that happened today

_____
_____
_____
_____

Something I learned today

_____
_____
_____
_____

Date : ...... / ...... / ......

My level of happiness

Mon Tue Wed Thu Fri Sat Sun
○ ○ ○ ○ ○ ○ ○

Today I'm thankful for

_____
_____
_____
_____
_____

Something awesome that happened today

_____
_____
_____

Something I learned today

_____
_____
_____
_____

Date : ...... / ...... / ......

Mon Tue Wed Thu Fri Sat Sun
○   ○   ○   ○   ○   ○   ○

My level of happiness

Today I'm thankful for

_____
_____
_____
_____
_____

Something awesome that happened today

_____
_____
_____

Something I learned today

_____
_____
_____
_____

Date : ...... / ...... / ......

Mon Tue Wed Thu Fri Sat Sun
○ ○ ○ ○ ○ ○ ○

My level of happiness

Today I'm thankful for

_____
_____
_____
_____
_____

Something awesome that happened today

_____
_____
_____

Something I learned today

_____
_____
_____
_____

Date : ...... / ...... / ......

Mon Tue Wed Thu Fri Sat Sun
○ ○ ○ ○ ○ ○ ○

My level of happiness

Today I'm thankful for

_____
_____
_____
_____
_____

Something awesome that happened today

_____
_____
_____

Something I learned today

_____
_____
_____
_____

Date : ...... / ...... / ......

Mon Tue Wed Thu Fri Sat Sun
 ○   ○   ○   ○   ○   ○   ○

My level of happiness

Today I'm thankful for

_____
_____
_____
_____
_____

Something awesome that happened today

_____
_____
_____

Something I learned today

_____
_____
_____
_____

Date : .... / .... / ....

Mon Tue Wed Thu Fri Sat Sun
 ○   ○   ○   ○   ○   ○   ○

My level of happiness

Today I'm thankful for

_____
_____
_____
_____
_____

Something awesome that happened today

_____
_____
_____

Something I learned today

_____
_____
_____
_____

Date : .... / .... / ....

Mon Tue Wed Thu Fri Sat Sun
 ○   ○   ○   ○   ○   ○   ○

Today I'm thankful for

_____

_____

_____

_____

_____

Something awesome that happened today

_____

_____

_____

Something I learned today

_____

_____

_____

_____

Date : ...... / ...... / ......

Mon Tue Wed Thu Fri Sat Sun
○   ○   ○   ○   ○   ○   ○

My level of happiness

Today I'm thankful for

_____
_____
_____
_____
_____

Something awesome that happened today

_____
_____
_____

Something I learned today

_____
_____
_____
_____

Date : .... / .... / ....

Mon Tue Wed Thu Fri Sat Sun
○   ○   ○   ○   ○   ○   ○

My level of happiness

Today I'm thankful for

_____

_____

_____

_____

_____

Something awesome that happened today

_____

_____

_____

Something I learned today

_____

_____

_____

_____

Date : ...... / ...... / ......

Mon Tue Wed Thu Fri Sat Sun
○ ○ ○ ○ ○ ○ ○

My level of happiness

Today I'm thankful for

Something awesome that happened today

Something I learned today

Date : ...... / ...... / ......

Mon Tue Wed Thu Fri Sat Sun
○   ○   ○   ○   ○   ○   ○

My level of happiness

Today I'm thankful for

Something awesome that happened today

Something I learned today

Date : .... / .... / ....

Mon Tue Wed Thu Fri Sat Sun
○ ○ ○ ○ ○ ○ ○

My level of happiness

Today I'm thankful for

_____
_____
_____
_____
_____

Something awesome that happened today

_____
_____
_____

Something I learned today

_____
_____
_____
_____

Date : .... / .... / ....

Mon Tue Wed Thu Fri Sat Sun
○   ○   ○   ○   ○   ○   ○

My level of happiness

Today I'm thankful for

_____

_____

_____

_____

_____

Something awesome that happened today

_____

_____

_____

Something I learned today

_____

_____

_____

_____

Date : ...... / ...... / ......

Mon Tue Wed Thu Fri Sat Sun
○ ○ ○ ○ ○ ○ ○

My level of happiness

Today I'm thankful for

_____
_____
_____
_____
_____

Something awesome that happened today

_____
_____
_____

Something I learned today

_____
_____
_____
_____

Date : ...... / ...... / ......

Mon Tue Wed Thu Fri Sat Sun
○ ○ ○ ○ ○ ○ ○

My level of happiness

Today I'm thankful for

_____
_____
_____
_____
_____

Something awesome that happened today

_____
_____
_____

Something I learned today

_____
_____
_____
_____

Date : ...... / ...... / ......

Mon Tue Wed Thu Fri Sat Sun
○   ○   ○   ○   ○   ○   ○

My level of happiness

Today I'm thankful for

_____
_____
_____
_____
_____

Something awesome that happened today

_____
_____
_____

Something I learned today

_____
_____
_____
_____

Date : ...... / ...... / ......

Mon Tue Wed Thu Fri Sat Sun
○   ○   ○   ○   ○   ○   ○

My level of happiness

Today I'm thankful for

_____
_____
_____
_____
_____

Something awesome that happened today

_____
_____
_____

Something I learned today

_____
_____
_____
_____

Date : ……. / ……. / …….

Mon Tue Wed Thu Fri Sat Sun
○   ○   ○   ○   ○   ○   ○

My level of happiness

Today I'm thankful for

_____
_____
_____
_____
_____

Something awesome that happened today

_____
_____
_____

Something I learned today

_____
_____
_____
_____

Date : ...... / ...... / ......

Mon Tue Wed Thu Fri Sat Sun
○ ○ ○ ○ ○ ○ ○

My level of happiness

Today I'm thankful for

_____
_____
_____
_____
_____
_____

Something awesome that happened today

_____
_____
_____

Something I learned today

_____
_____
_____
_____

Date : ...... / ...... / ......

Mon Tue Wed Thu Fri Sat Sun
 ○   ○   ○   ○   ○   ○   ○

Today I'm thankful for

_____

_____

_____

_____

_____

Something awesome that happened today

_____

_____

_____

Something I learned today

_____

_____

_____

_____

Date : ...... / ...... / ......

Mon Tue Wed Thu Fri Sat Sun
◯   ◯   ◯   ◯   ◯   ◯   ◯

My level of happiness

Today I'm thankful for

_____

_____

_____

_____

_____

Something awesome that happened today

_____

_____

_____

Something I learned today

_____

_____

_____

_____

Date : ...... / ...... / ......

Mon Tue Wed Thu Fri Sat Sun
○ ○ ○ ○ ○ ○ ○

My level of happiness

Today I'm thankful for

_____
_____
_____
_____
_____

Something awesome that happened today

_____
_____
_____

Something I learned today

_____
_____
_____
_____

Date : .... / .... / ....

Mon Tue Wed Thu Fri Sat Sun
○ ○ ○ ○ ○ ○ ○

My level of happiness

Today I'm thankful for

Something awesome that happened today

Something I learned today

Date : ...... / ...... / ......

Mon Tue Wed Thu Fri Sat Sun
○   ○   ○   ○   ○   ○   ○

My level of happiness

Today I'm thankful for

_____
_____
_____
_____
_____

Something awesome that happened today

_____
_____
_____

Something I learned today

_____
_____
_____
_____

Date : ...... / ...... / ......

Mon Tue Wed Thu Fri Sat Sun
○ ○ ○ ○ ○ ○ ○

My level of happiness

Today I'm thankful for

Something awesome that happened today

Something I learned today

Date : ...... / ...... / ......

Mon Tue Wed Thu Fri Sat Sun
 ○   ○   ○   ○   ○   ○   ○

My level of happiness

Today I'm thankful for

Something awesome that happened today

Something I learned today

Date : ...... / ...... / ......

Mon Tue Wed Thu Fri Sat Sun
○ ○ ○ ○ ○ ○ ○

My level of happiness

Today I'm thankful for

_____
_____
_____
_____
_____
_____

Something awesome that happened today

_____
_____
_____

Something I learned today

_____
_____
_____
_____

Date : ...... / ...... / ......

Mon Tue Wed Thu Fri Sat Sun
 ◯   ◯   ◯   ◯   ◯   ◯   ◯

My level of happiness

Today I'm thankful for

Something awesome that happened today

Something I learned today

Date : ...... / ...... / ......

Mon Tue Wed Thu Fri Sat Sun
○   ○   ○   ○   ○   ○   ○

My level of happiness

Today I'm thankful for

_____
_____
_____
_____
_____
_____

Something awesome that happened today

_____
_____
_____

Something I learned today

_____
_____
_____
_____

Date : ...... / ...... / ......

Mon Tue Wed Thu Fri Sat Sun
○ ○ ○ ○ ○ ○ ○

My level of happiness

Today I'm thankful for

Something awesome that happened today

Something I learned today

Date : ...... / ...... / ......

Mon Tue Wed Thu Fri Sat Sun
○ ○ ○ ○ ○ ○ ○

My level of happiness

Today I'm thankful for

_____
_____
_____
_____
_____

Something awesome that happened today

_____
_____
_____

Something I learned today

_____
_____
_____
_____

Notes

Notes

Made in the USA
Las Vegas, NV
09 August 2022